Cultural Crafts

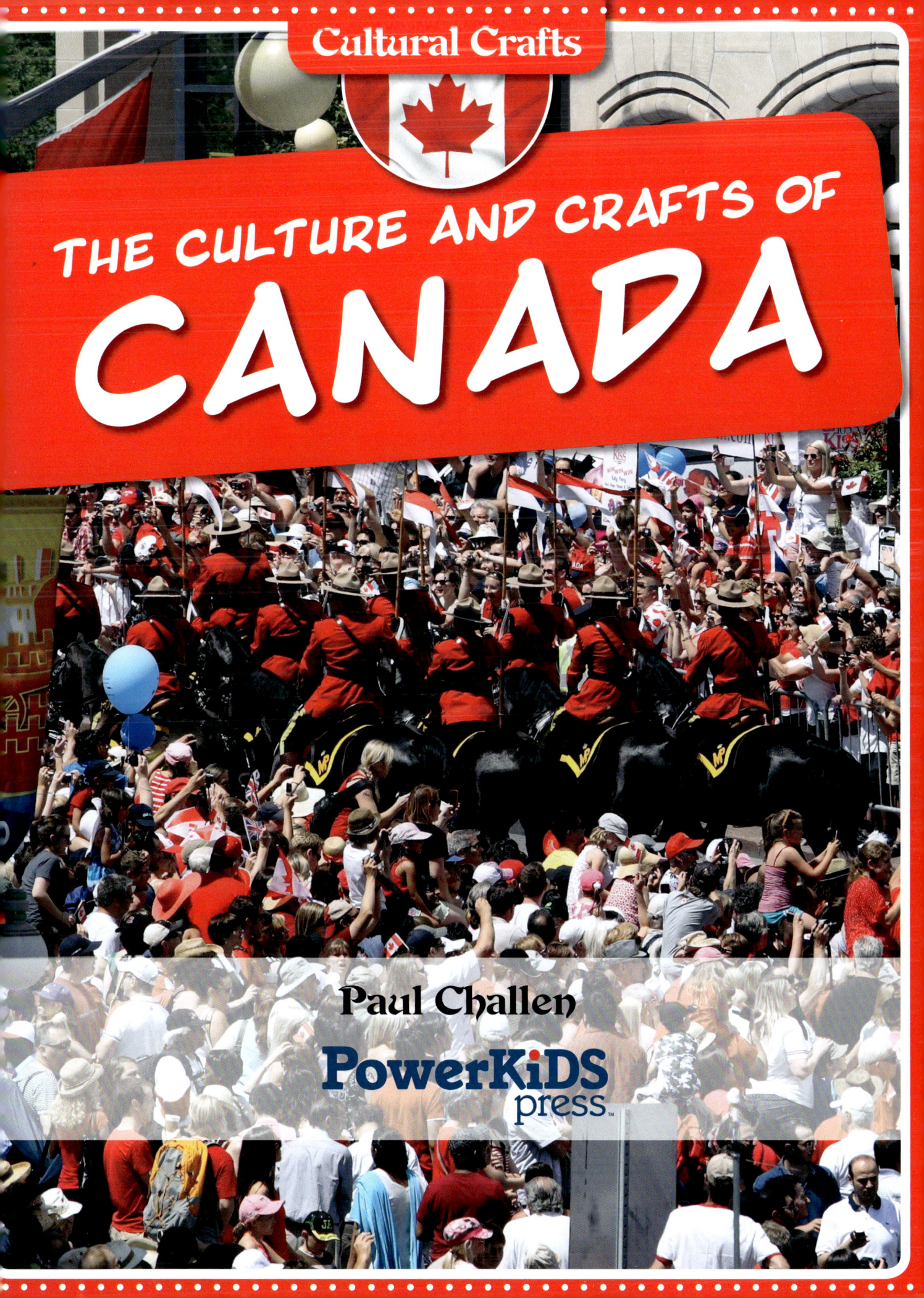

THE CULTURE AND CRAFTS OF CANADA

Paul Challen

PowerKiDS press

Published in 2016 by **The Rosen Publishing Group, Inc.**
29 East 21st Street, New York, NY 10010

Copyright © 2016 by The Rosen Publishing Group, Inc.

All rights reserved. No part of this book may be reproduced in any form without permission in writing from the publisher, except by a reviewer.

Developed and produced for Rosen by BlueAppleWorks Inc.

Art Director: T. J. Choleva
Managing Editor for BlueAppleWorks: Melissa McClellan
Designer: Joshua Avramson
Photo Research: Jane Reid
Editor: Rachel Stuckey
Craft Artisans: Jerrie McClellan (p. 7, 17), Sandor Monos (p. 21), Jane Yates (p. 25)

Special thanks to Sandor Monos, a renowned Canadian sculptor, for the inukshuk art.

Photo Credits:
Cover top left, p. 10 top, 11 bottom meunierd/Shutterstock; cover top middle left Natalia Pushchina/Shutterstock; cover top middle right Ariena/Shutterstock; cover top right bikeriderlondon; cover middle Joshua Avramson/Shutterstock images; cover bottom middle right, p. 9 right photokup/Shutterstock; cover bottom images left, middle left, right, p. 6–7, 16–17, 20–21, 24–25 Austen Photography; cover, title page top Marques/Shutterstock; back cover, p. 4 top Arid Ocean/Shutterstock; title page, p 8 top David P. Lewis/Shutterstock; p. 4 Jody Ann/Shutterstock; p. 5 left Click Images/Shutterstock; p. 5 middle, 8–9 Wangkun Jia/Dreamstime; p. 5 right Mike Clegg/Dreamstime; p. 9 Sergei Bachlakov/Dreamstime; p. 10 bottom meunierd/Shutterstock; p. 11 top Bhofack2/Dreamstime; p. 11 middle Rob Crandall/Shutterstock; p. 12 left, 12 top, 13 top left, 18 bottom Paul McKinnon/Shutterstock; p.13 top right, 13 bottom left, 13 bottom right Maridav/Shutterstock; p. 14–15 D. Gordon E. Robertson/Creative Commons; p. 14 left, 14 middle Norman Pogson/Shutterstock; p. 14 right, 29 left Jamie Roach/Dreamstime; p. 15 right Anusorn.Sutapan/Shutterstock; p. 18 top Tyler McKay/Shutterstock; p. 19 left, 19 right Ansgar Walk/Creative Commons; p. 22 top rmnoa357/Shutterstock; p. 22 bottom Max Topchii/Shutterstock; p. 23 top bikeriderlondon/Shutterstock; p. .23 bottom Mark Spowart/Dreamstime; p. 26 top Monkey Business Images/Shutterstock; p. 26 bottom Elena Elisseeva/Dreamstime; p. 27 left Sian Cox/Dreamstime; p. 27 middle Foodio /Shutterstock; p. 27 right Martine Oger/Dreamstime; p. 28 top Sergei Bachlakov/Shutterstock; p. 28 bottom photosthatrock /Shutterstock; p. 29 right Ipatov/Shutterstock.

Cataloging-in-Publication-Data

Challen, Paul.
The culture and crafts of Canada / by Paul Challen.
p. cm. — (Cultural crafts)
Includes index.
ISBN 978-1-4994-1118-8 (pbk.)
ISBN 978-1-4994-1128-7 (6 pack)
ISBN 978-1-4994-1155-3 (library binding)
1. Canada — Juvenile literature. 2. Canada — Social life and customs — Juvenile literature.
3. Handicraft — Juvenile literature. I. Challen, Paul C. (Paul Clarence), 1967-. II. Title.
F1008.2 C44 2016
971—d23

Manufactured in the United States of America
CPSIA Compliance Information: Batch #WS15PK: For Further Information contact: Rosen Publishing, New York, New York at 1-800-237-9932

Contents

The Country of Canada	4
Craft to Make – Loon	6
National Holidays	8
French Canadians	10
Winter Festivals	12
Scottish Heritage Festivals	14
Craft to Make – Scottish Hat	16
Celebrating Aboriginal Peoples	18
Craft to Make – Inukshuk	20
Traditional Clothing	22
Craft to Make – The Mountie Hat	24
Canadian Cuisine	26
Favorite Sports in Canada	28
Glossary	30
For More Information	31
Index	32

The Country of Canada

Canada is a large country on the continent of North America. It is the second biggest country in the world, but has a population of only 35 million people. There are more people living in the state of California. The country is divided into **provinces** and **territories**. Ottawa is the capital city of Canada, but the largest city is Toronto. Canada is a democracy, meaning the citizens elect their government. However, Queen Elizabeth II is the official head of state and appoints a Governor General to represent her in Canada.

The beaver is the national animal of Canada. It appears on the 5-cent coin.

Cultural Mosaic

Canada is a country of many cultures. **Aboriginal peoples** have lived in Canada for many hundreds of years. The first immigrants came from France and England beginning in the 1600s. After the original arrival of the French in the 16th century, there were many Irish and Scottish settlers, especially in Canada's eastern provinces.

Today, Canadians come from many parts of the world. Canada is known around the world as a "**cultural mosaic.**" There are many different religions practiced in Canada. French and English are the official languages of Canada, but Canadians also speak many different languages from all over the world.

The Changing of the Guard on Parliament Hill is a popular attraction in Ottawa. Other formal military uniforms show Canada's English and Scottish heritage.

The CN Tower in Toronto is one of the best-known Canadian landmarks.

Craft to Make

The loon is a well-known Canadian bird. The loon spends as much time swimming on the surface of lakes and rivers as it does in the air. The Canadian $1 coin is known as a "loonie" because a picture of this popular bird is on one face of the coin. The $2 coin is called a "toonie."

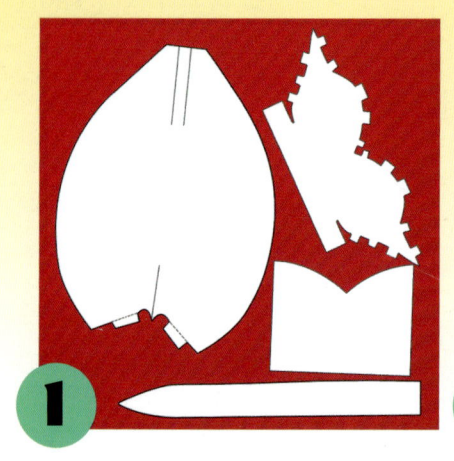

1 Trace the patterns found on page 31. Trace around the pattern on black cardstock using a light colored pencil.

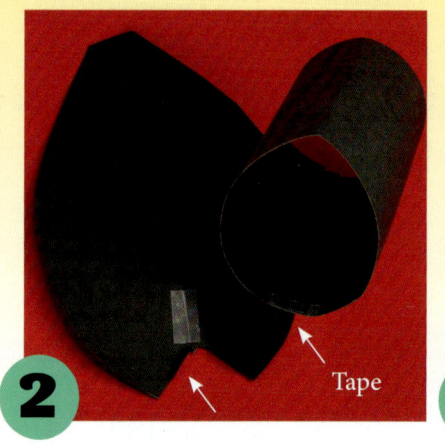

2 Make the indicated cuts on the body piece. Fold the tabs down. Next to the tabs, overlap the cut paper and tape in place. Cut a rectangle piece of cardstock that is 5½ by 8 inches (14 x 20.5 cm). Roll this into a tube and tape it together. Bend it gently to make it more oval.

3 Glue or tape the body over the tube. Paint white dots on the body with white paint. Paint white dots on the two wings cut out in Step 1. Glue the wings to the body.

You'll Need

- Black cardstock
- White colored pencil
- Scissors
- Tape or glue
- White paint
- Brush

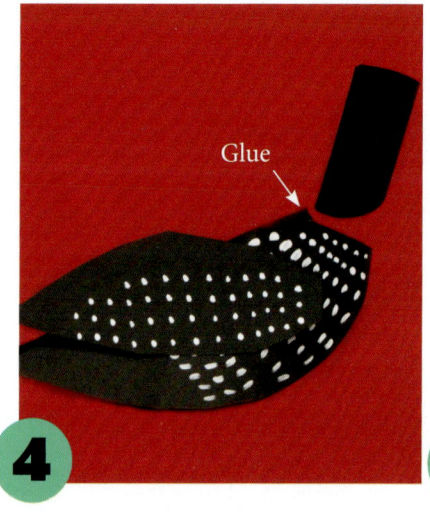

4 Bend the neck piece so both ends meet and glue or tape in place. Put glue on the body tabs. Press the neck to the tabs.

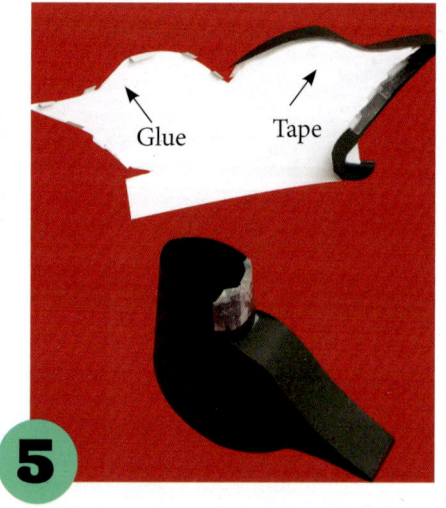

5 Fold the tabs on the head piece. Tape the middle head piece to the tabs on the right side. Fold the left side over and glue the tabs to the middle part. Glue or tape the neck piece together.

Loon

6

Put some glue on the inside of the neck at the top. Fit the head into the neck. Paint a white band around the neck, and under the chin. Paint eyes on each side of the head.

7

National Holidays

Canadians celebrate many national holidays throughout the year. On national holidays, most people get a day off because schools, offices, banks, and many stores are closed. Some of the national holidays in Canada include traditional Christian celebrations like Christmas and Easter. However, schools and workplaces allow people of different faiths to take days off for major religious holidays such as **Yom Kippur** and **Eid**.

Canada Day is always celebrated on July 1. Remembrance Day is observed on November 11 and honors those who have served Canada in the military. Canadians also enjoy a holiday in May to celebrate Queen Victoria's birthday and Quebec residents celebrate Saint-Jean-Baptiste Day in June.

While they are not official holidays, Canadians also celebrate Valentine's Day, St. Patrick's Day, Father's Day, Mother's Day, and Halloween.

Grand parades are held all over Canada to celebrate Canada's birthday on July 1st.

Canada's Birthday

Canada's national holiday is called Canada Day. Canada Day is always on July 1. It was on this day in 1867 that three British colonies formed the country of Canada. Canada Day was known as Dominion Day until the 1980s, when Canada became fully independent of the United Kingdom.

Canadians celebrate their country's birthday with parades, picnics, multicultural events, and grand fireworks displays.

Ceremonies for new citizens are often held on Canada Day.

Canada Flag Craft

The maple leaf has been used as a Canadian emblem since the 1700s. But the familiar red and white maple leaf flag was first used in 1965. Now the National Flag of Canada, the "Maple Leaf" has two red sections and a white section in the middle. There is a red 11-point maple leaf in the center of the white section.

Use these instructions to make your own National Flag of Canada.

- If you can, collect red maple leaves during the fall. Or, cut your own out of red paper.
- Cut a flag-shaped sheet of white cardstock paper.
- Use glue to attach the leaves to each end of the cardstock, like in the image below. Leave the center of the cardstock white. Attach the biggest and best leaf to the center.

Use your flag to celebrate Canada Day on July 1.

French Canadians

Quebec City is the capital of Quebec, Canada's biggest province.

Many of the first settlers in Canada came from France to farm and trap animals for fur. Many of these people settled in the eastern province of Quebec. Even when Quebec became a British colony, it retained its French culture. There are also large French-speaking communities throughout Canada, especially in the Maritime provinces of New Brunswick and Nova Scotia.

French Canadians are the second largest ethnic group after Canadians of English origin. French Canadians are one of the country's three founding nations, along with English Canadians and First Nations people.

French Canadians are proud of their heritage. The provincial motto of Quebec is *Je me souviens*, which means "I remember."

French-Canadian Culture

French Canadians are the largest group of Francophones or French-speakers in North America. French is the official language in Quebec and there is a special law that requires French to be the primary language of business and education. French is also an official language in the province of New Brunswick. In Canada, federal government affairs are conducted in both French and English.

Other aspects of French-Canadian culture include unique foods, folk music, storytelling, and traditional costumes. *La fête nationale* is a provincial holiday in Quebec celebrated on June 24, the Catholic feast day of St. John the Baptist. Traditionally a religious holiday, Saint-Jean-Baptiste Day is now as big a holiday in Quebec as Canada Day is in the rest of the country. On June 24, French Canadians celebrate French culture with parades and festivities.

DID YOU KNOW?

Poutine is a Canadian dish that was invented in Quebec in the 1950s. To make it, start with French fries, top them with cheese curds and then gravy for a messy-but-yummy treat. Poutine is served all over Canada and is starting to catch on in other parts of the world.

On Saint-Jean-Baptiste Day, Quebecers and other French Canadians celebrate the French-Canadian culture.

11

Winter Festivals

When the Rideau Canal in Ottawa freezes over, it becomes the world's largest skating rink.

Ice sculptors create fantastic ice sculptures during winter festivals.

Most of Canada is quite cold in the winter—but Canadians don't let that stop them from having fun! **Winter carnivals** with snow and ice sports, music, and hot treats and drinks are popular in many parts of the country.

Winterlude Winter festival is held in Ottawa, Canada's capital city. At Winterlude you can enjoy ice carvings and snow sculptures, a gigantic snow playground, and many performances under the winter sky. Ottawa's biggest winter attraction is skating on the Rideau Canal—a **UNESCO** World Heritage Site and the world's largest skating rink!

Carnival in Quebec

The most famous of winter festivals is *Carnaval de Quebec*, or the Quebec Winter Carnival, which is held in Quebec City. The Winter Carnival is the oldest of Canada's winter festivals. More than a million people visit Winter Carnival each year to take part in skating, tobogganing, snowshoeing, and other fun winter activities. As well, the event features giant, spectacular sculptures carved out of hardened snow and ice.

Winter Snowshoes

Snowshoes were used by the early fur trappers in Canada to get around in winter. Now they are a fun way to enjoy the snow. Snowshoes are made of a wide wooden base with webbing. The webbed surface allows the wearer to walk on top of thick snow without sinking in.

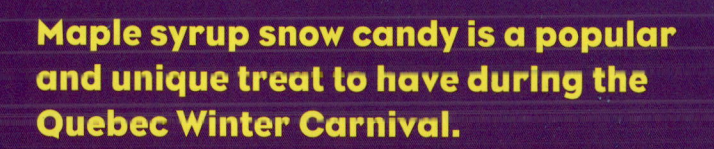

Maple syrup snow candy is a popular and unique treat to have during the Quebec Winter Carnival.

Bonhomme Carnaval is the mascot of the winter carnival. *Bonhomme de neige* means "snowman" in French.

The International Ice Canoe Race on the St. Lawrence River is the main event of *Carnaval de Quebec*.

13

Scottish Heritage Festivals

Haggis is a dish made of sheep's organs seasoned with minced onions and spices, cooked in sheep's stomach.

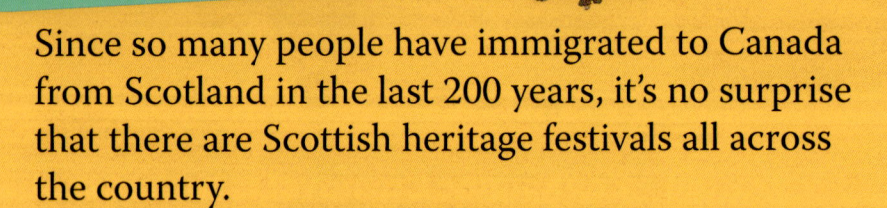

Since so many people have immigrated to Canada from Scotland in the last 200 years, it's no surprise that there are Scottish heritage festivals all across the country.

Also known as **Highland Games**, these events feature sports such as caber tossing, weight throwing, and Scottish hammer tossing. Scottish music—including songs played on the famous bagpipes—highland dancing, and classic Scots dishes such as haggis are also common at these festivals.

The caber toss is a traditional Scottish athletic event in which competitors toss a large pole called a "caber."

DID YOU KNOW

Canada has its own tartans, which are patterns used in woven cloth. Tartans were first brought to Canada by Scottish settlers. Almost every province and territory also has its own official tartan. In 1956, Nova Scotia became the first province to officially adopt its own tartan. Canada's tartans are officially recognized in Scotland too. Canada's national tartan is known as the maple leaf tartan and has been an official national symbol since 2011.

Bagpipes and traditional Scottish dancing add to the fun at Highland Games festivals.

World Famous Highland Games

Two of the most famous Scottish festivals are the ones held in Kincardine and Maxville, Ontario. The festival in Maxville is known as the Glengarry Highland Games and has been held for more than 50 years. Around 50,000 people attend each year. That makes it one of the biggest Scottish heritage festivals outside of Scotland!

Craft to Make

The traditional Scottish hat, or "tam," is still popular in Canada today. It features a soft, brimless cap with a tartan design and a pom-pom on top.

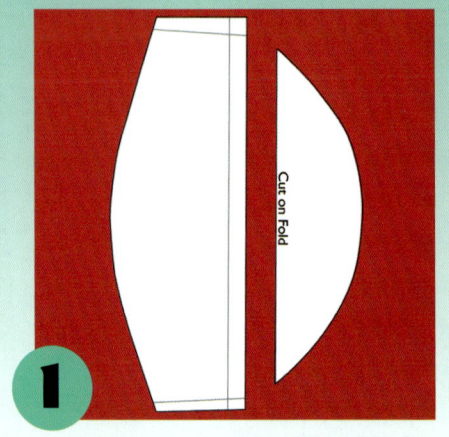

1 Trace the patterns found on page 30. Fold the poster board in half. Trace around the pattern of the base of the hat at the fold line. using a light colored pencil. Move the pattern down 1/2 inch (1.3 cm) and trace the top of the hat again. Trace the top part of the hat on the fold line. Cut out the pieces.

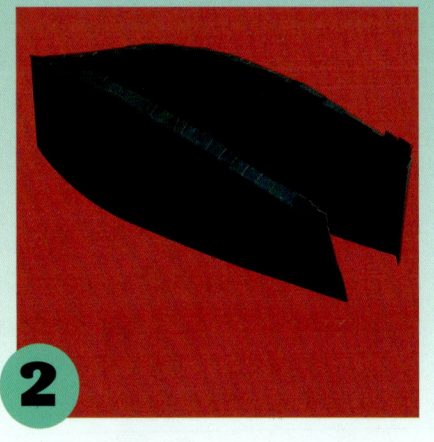

2 Cut a 1/2 inch (1.3 cm) fringe to the second line all along the top, or rounded, edge of base piece. Bend the fringes down. Fold ½ inch of one end to make a tab.

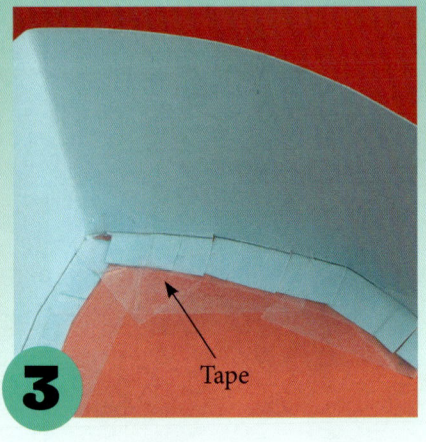

3 Line up the base piece with the top of the hat. Using small amounts of tape, tape the tabs to the top on the inside. (The photo uses different colored paper so it is more visible.)

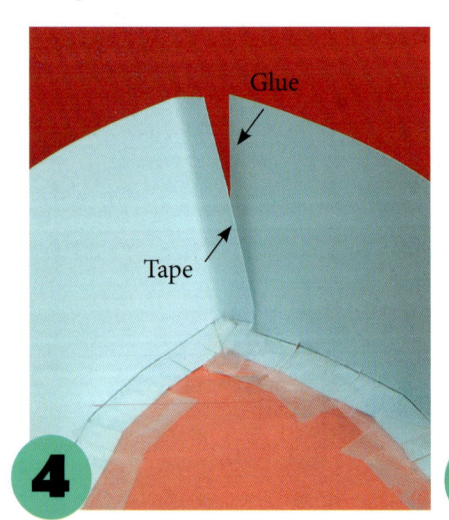

4 Put glue along the outside of the tab and tape on the inside to hold the two ends together.

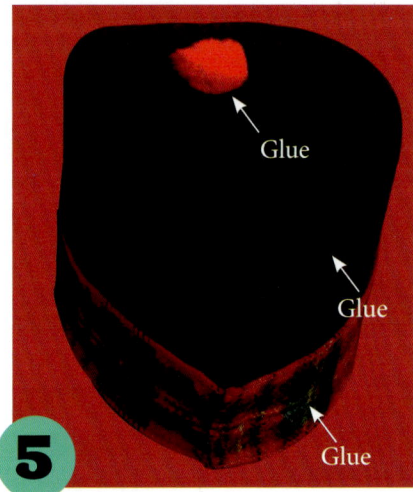

5 Apply glue all around the outside edges. Glue a ribbon to the hat at the bottom of the base. Glue a pom-pom to the top of the hat.

You'll Need

- Black poster board
- Colored pencil
- Scissors
- Glue
- Tape
- Ribbon (plaid or red)
- Black ribbon
- Red pom-pom
- Stapler

Scottish Hat

6

Cut one 21-inch (53.3 cm) piece of ribbon. Cut one 7-inch (17.8 cm) piece. Fold the short piece so the ends meet and staple them together. Fold the long ribbon so that one end is longer than the other. Put the short ribbon through the loop. Fold the loop over and staple it to the back of the hat.

17

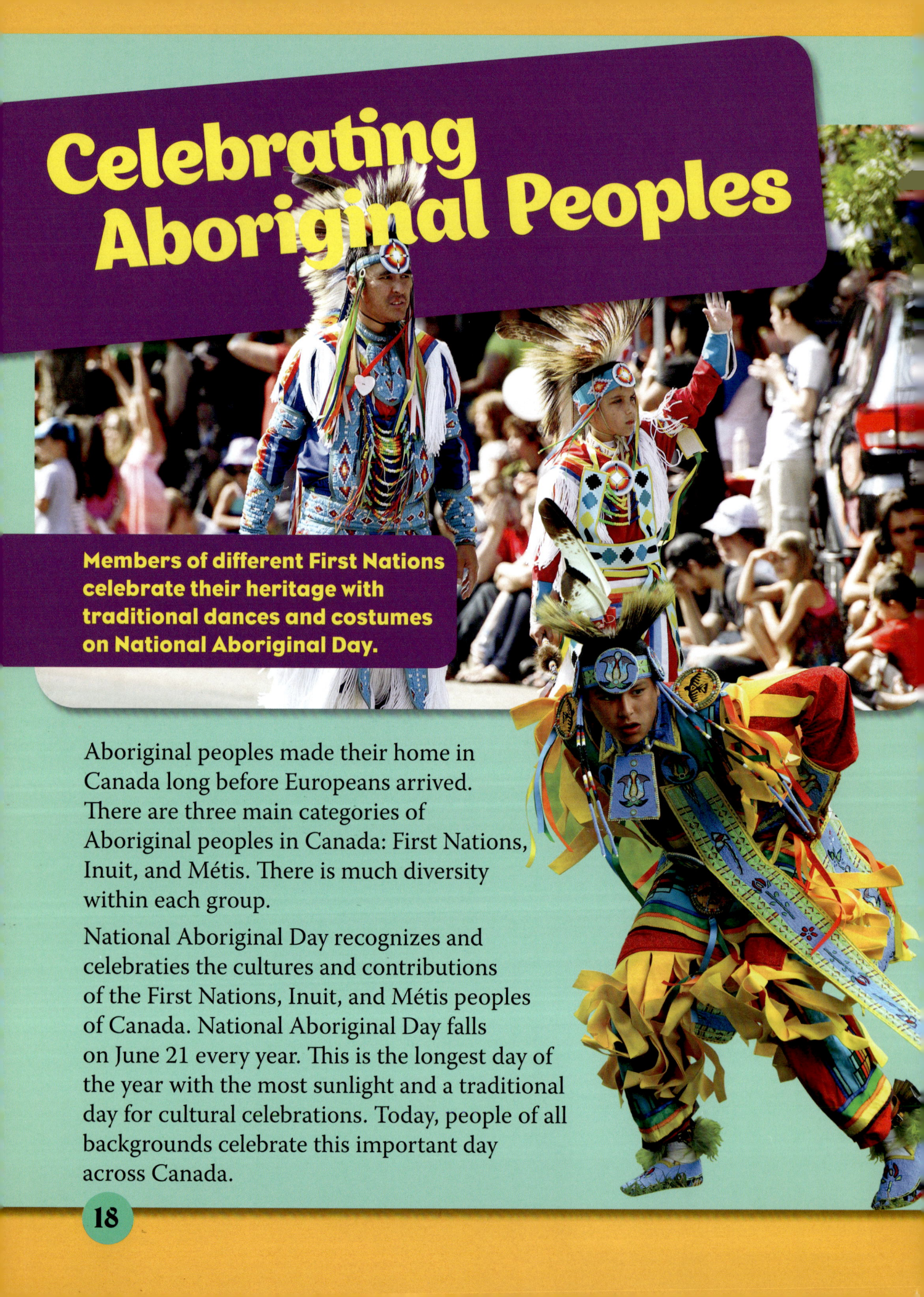

Celebrating Aboriginal Peoples

Members of different First Nations celebrate their heritage with traditional dances and costumes on National Aboriginal Day.

Aboriginal peoples made their home in Canada long before Europeans arrived. There are three main categories of Aboriginal peoples in Canada: First Nations, Inuit, and Métis. There is much diversity within each group.

National Aboriginal Day recognizes and celebraties the cultures and contributions of the First Nations, Inuit, and Métis peoples of Canada. National Aboriginal Day falls on June 21 every year. This is the longest day of the year with the most sunlight and a traditional day for cultural celebrations. Today, people of all backgrounds celebrate this important day across Canada.

Canada's Aboriginal Peoples

The First Nations are the largest Aboriginal group in Canada. Mi'kmaq, Ojibwa, Cree, Dene, Salish, and Haida are just some of the many First Nation ethnic groups. Each ethnic group has many bands, nations, or tribes—there are about 630 bands recognized by the Canadian government. While European colonists destroyed their lifestyle and culture, the First Nations are now rebuilding their communities and way of life.

The Inuit live in Canada's north, and are well-adapted to living in the Arctic. The Inuit hunt seals, whales, and cold-water fish for food and other resources like fur and oil.

The Inuit also hunt large animals like elk and caribou that live in Canada's northern climates. Inuit people have traditionally built homes out of blocks of ice—known as igloos.

The Métis people are a distinct ethnic group descended from European **fur traders** and their First Nation wives. The Métis people created their own unique culture and language. Louis Riel was a famous Métis leader in the 1800s who helped found the province of Manitoba. He also fought to protect Métis rights.

Welcome to Canada!

In 1999 Canada welcomed a new addition to the Confederation. The territory of Nunavut was created in the eastern part of the Northwest Territories and became the newest part of Canada. Nunavut is Canada's largest territory and includes most of Canada's Arctic lands. There are only about 30,000 people living in Nunavut, and most of them are Inuit. Nunavut's capital is Iqaluit. The name Nunavut means "our land" in the Inuktitut language. Nunavut has no political parties and the elected representatives use **consensus** to select ministers and decide on an **agenda**.

Many Inuit people still hunt in traditional ways. However, most wear modern clothes and use snowmobiles instead of dog teams.

19

Craft to Make

The inukshuk is a traditional Inuit stone marker. Made from rocks and stones, an inukshuk is intended to give directions to travelers. The stone markers come in all sizes. The larger ones are assembled by teams of people.

1 Gather an assortment of rocks. Look for flat rocks as well as oval rocks. Wash the rocks with soapy water. Rinse and leave to dry.

2 Arrange your rocks into the shape of a figure on a piece of cardboard.

3 Choose a large flat rock to be the base. Add the rocks that will be the legs. Use small bits of modeling clay to keep them in place.

Balance each layer

4 Add more rocks, balancing each layer in place as you go. Turn the piece of cardboard, to see how the inukshuk looks from all sides.

5 You can also buy polished stones to build an inukshuk. Repeat the steps above with these rocks. Add glue to help secure the rocks.

You'll Need

Rocks
Cardboard
Modeling clay
Glue

Inukshuk

21

Traditional Clothing

Because many parts of Canada have winter weather for several months of the year, much of the traditional clothing worn by Canadians is cold-weather gear.

The toque is the most iconic piece of clothing in Canada. This winter hat, usually made of wool, has become popular as a year-round fashion statement. But as well as looking good, toques are also excellent for keeping the head warm. They come in different shapes, from close-fitting to large and pointy with a pom-pom on top.

Toques and parkas are worn by many Canadians during cold winter months.

Warm and Comfy

A parka is a large, winter coat. Parkas have hoods, often lined with fur or synthetic fur. A traditional parka is knee-length, and because of the way they are designed and padded, they are extremely warm. The first parkas were made by the Inuit people out of the skins of animals they had caught. The parka was an ideal coat for hunting and fishing in the frozen weather of the Canadian north, and is now popular around the world.

Traditional Inuit parkas gave way to modern fabrics and designs.

The Royal Canadian Mounted Police

The Royal Canadian Mounted Police, or RCMP, was founded in 1920. As their name suggests, the RCMP rode horses. That is where they got their nickname, the "Mounties." Today, only some RCMP officers still ride horses as part of their duties. But the name hasn't changed. The RCMP still dress in their traditional uniforms featuring their distinctive red jackets. But they are also a fully modern national police force responsible for fighting crime across Canada.

The Royal Canadian Mounted Police are one of the most recognizable police forces in the world.

Craft to Make

The mounties are well known for their distinctive brimmed hats. These hats are great for keeping out snow, sun, and rain.

1. Draw a square shape on a piece of cardboard with sides measuring 13 inches (30.5 cm). Draw diagonal lines from corner to corner to pinpoint the center of the square. Draw and cut out a 13-inch (30.5 cm) circle from the cardboard.

2. Draw a 6-inch (15.25 cm) circle around the center. Draw a 5-inch (13 cm) circle inside the 6-inch circle. Mark lines connecting the circles as shown above. Cut the smaller circle out. Cut along the lines just reaching the edges of the larger circle to form tabs. Lift the tabs up.

3. Draw and cut out a 21-inch (53.3 cm) by 3½-inch (9 cm) rectangle from white poster board to make the side band of the hat. Place the side band inside the circle of the cardboard base and tape the two ends together. Remove from the base.

You'll Need

- Cardboard
- White poster board
- Masking tape
- Newspaper
- Plastic wrap
- Glue water
- Paper strips
- Sandpaper
- Light brown paint
- Brush
- Dark brown ribbon or construction paper

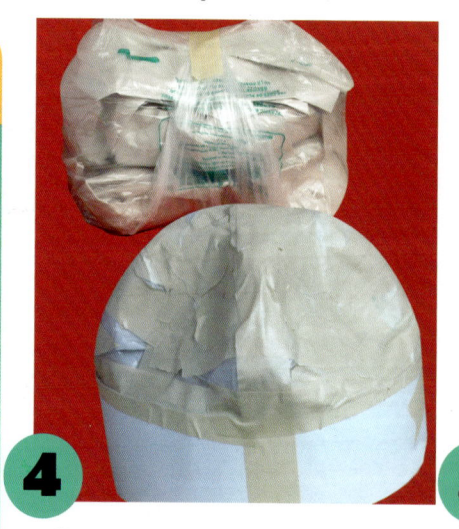

4. Fill a plastic bag with newspaper. Squish the air out and roll it so the shape fits into the side band. Tape it all around. Squish four indents into the top. Hold the indents in place and tape. Tape the band to the newspaper form.

5. Cover in plastic wrap. Put white glue in a container. Add a little water to dilute it. Dip paper strips in the glue. Squeeze off the excess with your fingers. Apply the strips to the hat form. Continue until it is covered. Have some strips extend over the bottom.

24

··The Mountie Hat

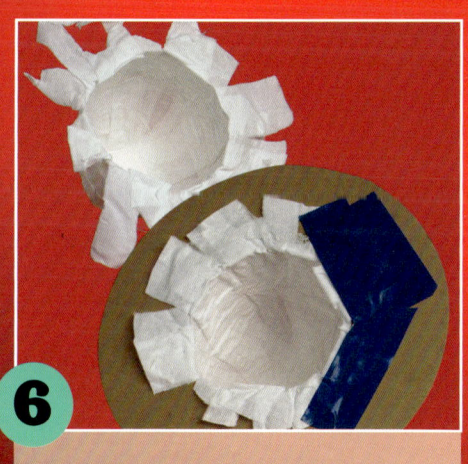

6 After the hat form dries, open the plastic bag and remove the paper. Pull the plastic and cardboard out. Put the top of the hat through the cardboard base and tape the extra strips to the base.

7 Optional: Sand the surface with fine sandpaper until it is smooth. Paint the hat. Glue a ribbon, or a strip of brown construction paper, around the base.

Paint

25

Canadian Cuisine

Many Canadians enjoy roast turkey meals during Christmas and Thanksgiving celebrations.

Living in such a multicultural society, most Canadians are used to eating food from around the world.

But Canada also has its own cuisine. Poutine (see page 11) is a popular dish from Quebec. But a more traditional French Canadian dish is tourtiére, a pie filled with meats such as beef, pork, or wild game, and often potatoes and onions as well.

Tourtiére is traditionally part of Christmas and New Year's Eve meals in Quebec.

Sweet and Delicious

A Canadian dessert classic is the butter tart, which combines a sweet filling with raisins inside a flaky crust. The filling is made with butter, sugar, and eggs. When the tart is baked just right, the filling becomes crunchy on top.

Of course, you cannot talk about Canadian food without mentioning maple syrup. Made by boiling the sweet sap of a maple tree, this syrup is very popular on top of pancakes, French toast, and ice cream.

Maple trees are tapped in early spring to collect their sap.

Montreal Smoked Meat

The city of Montreal in Quebec is home to a specially prepared type of beef. The makers of this meat rub it with a special combination of spices before using a special technique called "smoking" to cook it. Montreal smoked meat is typically served in restaurants called delicatessens—or delis. This meat is most popular in sandwiches and can be found all over Canada. One of the most popular places to get smoked meat is Schwartz's Deli in Montreal.

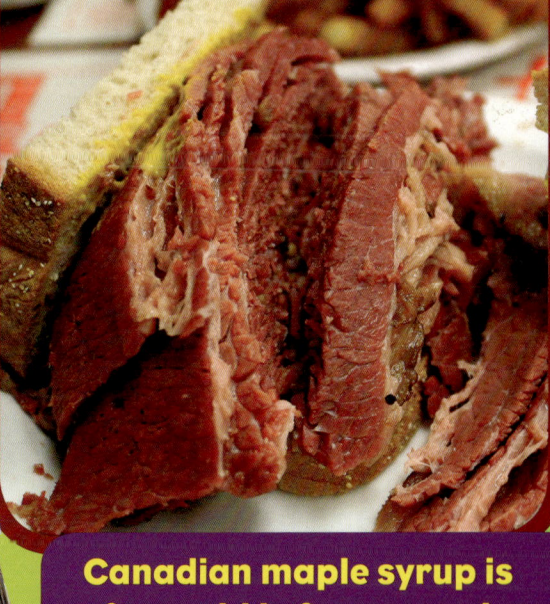

Canadian maple syrup is often sold in fancy maple leaf–shaped bottles.

Favorite Sports in Canada

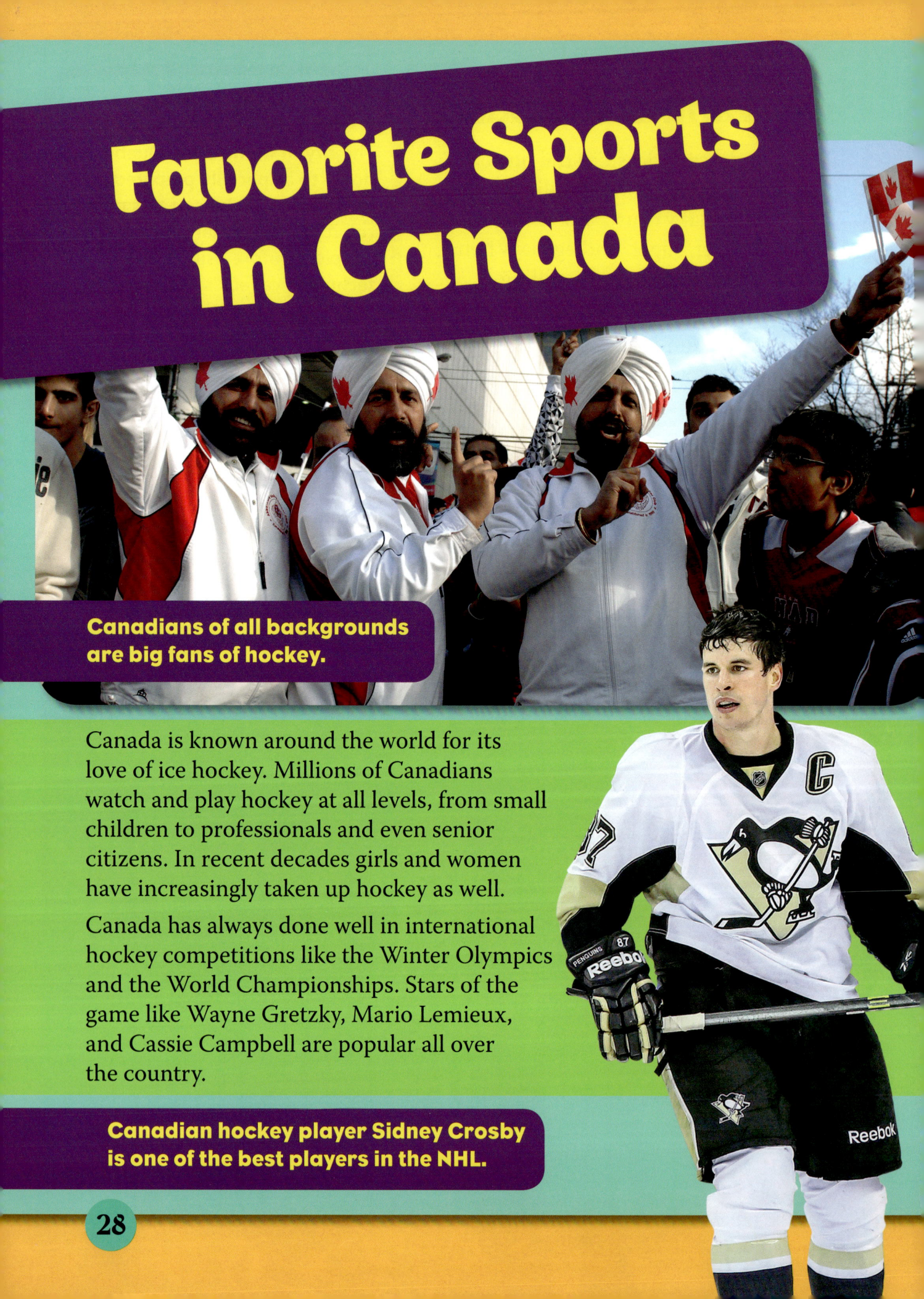

Canadians of all backgrounds are big fans of hockey.

Canada is known around the world for its love of ice hockey. Millions of Canadians watch and play hockey at all levels, from small children to professionals and even senior citizens. In recent decades girls and women have increasingly taken up hockey as well.

Canada has always done well in international hockey competitions like the Winter Olympics and the World Championships. Stars of the game like Wayne Gretzky, Mario Lemieux, and Cassie Campbell are popular all over the country.

Canadian hockey player Sidney Crosby is one of the best players in the NHL.

Sporty Nation

Although Canada is best known for hockey, many other sports are popular there too. The official national sport is actually the traditional Aboriginal game of **lacrosse**. The Scottish game of curling is very popular as well. The first Canadian curling club was founded in Montreal in 1807. In curling, players slide 40-pound (18 kg) stones known as "rocks" down a long sheet of ice toward a bull's-eye target. They use brooms to brush the ice and affect the path of the rock.

Canadians also play soccer, baseball, football, and tennis—just to name a few. And of course, winter activities like skating and skiing are also very popular.

DID YOU KNOW?

Basketball was invented by a Canadian, Dr. James Naismith. Naismith was looking for a game his physical education students could play indoors during the winter. Today, basketball is played on both outdoor and indoor courts. In recent years, some top international stars of the sport, like Steve Nash, have been Canadian.

Curling is a game of focus and concentration.

Skiing and snowboarding are part of winter fun in Canada.

29

GLOSSARY

Aboriginal peoples The native people of Canada.

agenda A set of policies or issues to be addressed by an individual or group.

consensus General agreement.

cultural mosaic A term used to describe Canadian society's multicultural makeup.

Eid The feast marking the end of the fast of Ramadan. Ramadan is the ninth month of the Islamic calendar; Muslims worldwide observe this as a month of fasting.

fur traders Men who hunt and trap animals and trade their furs.

Highland Games A festival of sports and culture that celebrates Scottish heritage.

lacrosse A game in which two 10-member teams try to send a small ball into each other's netted goal with a crosse or stick, at the end of which is a netted pocket for catching, carrying, or throwing the ball.

province One of the main geographical divisions of Canada. There are 10 provinces in Canada.

territory One of the main geographical divisions of Canada. There are three territories in Canada.

UNESCO An agency of the United Nations that promotes education, communication, and arts around the world.

Winter carnival A festival held in the cold months of the year featuring sports, food and drink, and music.

Yom Kippur A Jewish holiday observed in September or October during which Jewish people do not eat or drink anything and pray to ask for forgiveness for mistakes made during the past year.

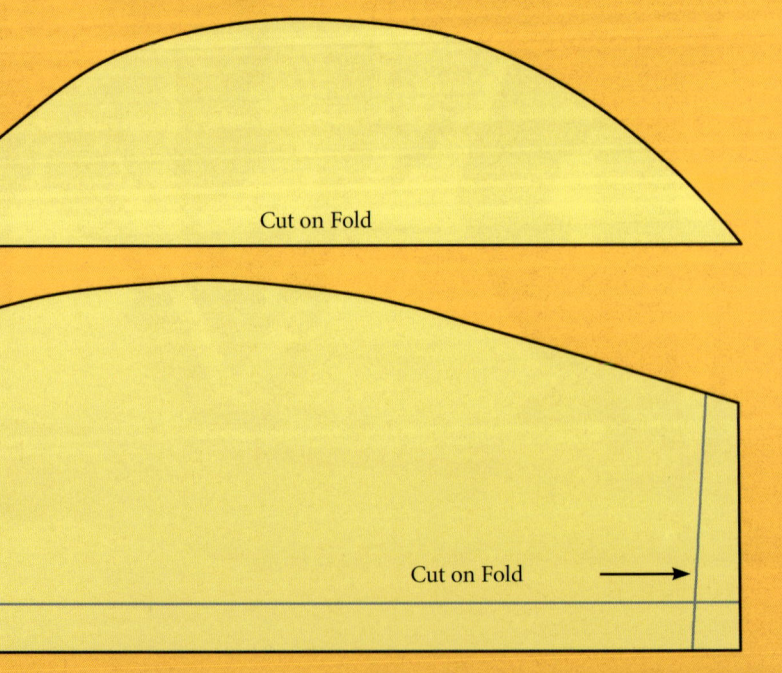

Cut on Fold

Cut on Fold

FOR MORE INFORMATION

Further Reading

Bowers, Vivien. *Wow Canada!: Exploring This Land from Coast to Coast to Coast.* Toronto, ON: Owlkids Books, 2010.

Hurley, Michael. *Countries Around the World: Canada.* Portsmouth, NH: Heinemann Publishing, 2014.

Kalman, Bobbie. *Canada: The Culture.* St. Catharines, ON: Crabtree Pub Co., 2009.

Sonneborn, Liz. *Canada.* New York, NY: Scholastic, 2011.

Websites

Due to the changing nature of Internet links, PowerKids Press has developed an online list of websites related to the subject of this book. This site is updated regularly. Please use this link to access the list:
www.powerkidslinks.com/cc/canada

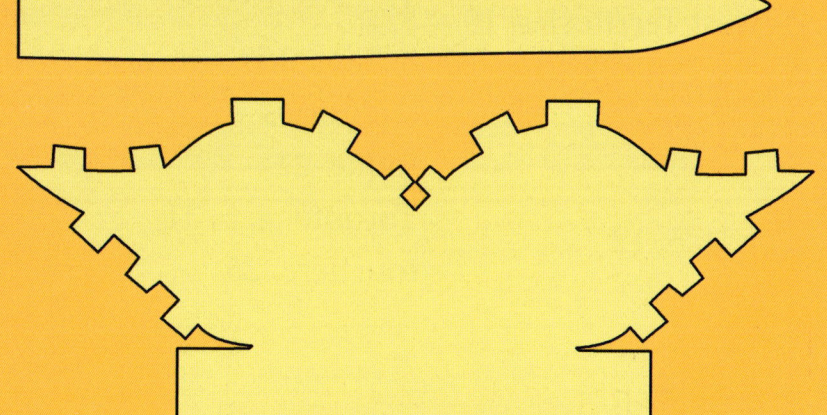

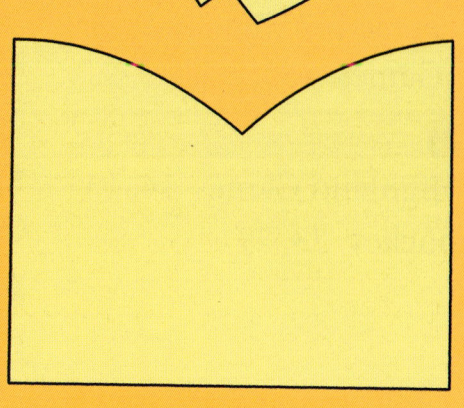

Note: Templates on pages 30-31 are scaled to 50 percent of the original size. Use a scanner or a printer to resize the templates. (200%)

INDEX

A
Aboriginal peoples 5, 18
Arctic 19

B
beaver 4

C
Canada Day 8, 9, 11
CN Tower 5
Crosby, Sidney 28
curling 29

E
England 5
English Canadians 10
Europeans 18

F
First Nations 10, 18, 19
France 5, 10
French Canadians 3, 10, 11

G
Glengarry Highland Games 15

H
Highland Games 14, 15
hockey 28, 29

I
igloos 19
Inuit 18, 19, 20, 23
inukshuk 20
Iqaluit 19

L
lacrosse 29
loon 6

M
Manitoba 19
maple leaf 9, 15, 27
maple syrup 13, 27
Métis 18, 19
Montreal 27, 29
Mountie Hat 25

N
Naismith, Dr. James 29
National Aboriginal Day 18
New Brunswick 10, 11
Northwest Territories 19
Nova Scotia 10, 15
Nunavut 19

O
Ottawa 4, 5, 12

P
parkas 22, 23
Parliament Hill 5
poutine 11, 26
provinces 4, 5, 10

Q
Quebec 8, 10, 11, 13, 26, 27
Quebec City 10, 13
Quebec Winter Carnival 13
Queen Elizabeth II 4

R
religions 5
Remembrance Day 8
Rideau Canal 12
Riel, Louis 19
Royal Canadian Mounted Police (RCMP) 23

S
Saint-Jean-Baptiste Day 8, 11
Scottish Hat 16, 17
snowmobiles 19
snowshoes 13

T
tartans 15
territories 4
toque 22
Toronto 4, 5, 31
tourtiére 26